D0475246

WILD ANIMALS

Trace Taylor & Gina Zorzi

At American Reading Company, we believe that reading success is the cornerstone of society-wide successes, both large and small. We believe the way to open a child to the possibilities of the world is through the power of books. To that end, our goal is to enable children to read—independently—for an hour each day. We are a resource to help schools and teachers accomplish that goal swiftly and effectively.

Our most notable program, 100 Book Challenge,° is our own proprietary independent reading program that has helped schools all over the country dramatically improve reading scores among their students, regardless of reading level.

Editor: Jane Hileman
Designer: Gareth Harte and Alex Alesio
Additional Contributors: judepics, catfish ball photograph, page 7

First Edition, February 2006
Second Edition, July 2009

ISBN: 978-1-59301-436-0, 1-59301-436-8

www.americanreading.com

WILD ANIMALS

Trace Taylor & Gina Zorzi

duck

pig

snake

sheep

monkey

fish

bear

frog

dog

zebra

giraffe

lion

Wild Animals Facts

Prairie Dogs (cover): Prairie Dogs are not really dogs. They are actually related to mice and rats. They are called dogs because they bark to warn each other about danger. Prairie dogs burrow into the earth, digging tunnels where they live in large underground communities.

The Bearded Pig: Bearded pigs are clever animals. In addition to digging up food like earthworms and roots, these pigs follow monkeys around so that they can eat the fruit that these monkeys drop from the trees high above.

Giraffe (title page): Giraffes' long necks help them reach high into the trees for leaves to eat. Their favorite snacks are the leaves that grow on the acacia tree. When baby giraffes are born, they already have their horns. These horns are made of bone, covered in hair and get bigger as the giraffe grows.

Snakes: Snakes are part of a family of cold-blooded animals called reptiles. This means that they depend on the sun to keep their bodies warm. Snakes can be found in many places including deserts, rain forests, woodlands, swamps, mountains, oceans, lakes, rivers, and even in cities. They like to eat mice, rats, birds, lizards, other snakes, small rodents and eggs.

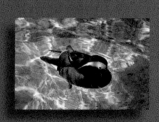

Mandarin Duck: While Mandarin Ducks are from Asia, other kinds of ducks can be found all over the world. All ducks are great swimmers because their webbed feet help them glide through the water. A duck's feathers also protect them from the cold water in the rivers, lakes, ponds and swamps where they swim.

Big Horned Sheep: All Big Horn sheep have horns, but male sheep have the biggest ones. Male sheep fight each other for control of the group by running into each other with their horns. These fights can last as long as a whole day, until one of the sheep finally gives up.

All the pictures in this book were taken at the Philadelphia Zoo in Philadelphia, Pennsylvania and at the Elmwood Zoo in Norristown, Pennsylvania. At the zoo you can see animals from all over the world. Many animals are endangered in their native homes and have trouble finding safe places to live outside of zoos. If you want to know more about endangered animals, visit a zoo near you. http://www.philadelphiazoo.org/

Panamanian Golden Frog: This poisonous frog lives in the rainforest of Panama. Male Panamanian golden frogs dance to attract female frogs. Like many frogs, this frog is in danger of totally disappearing because of pollution. Since frogs breathe through their skin, they can absorb this air pollution and get sick or die.

African Wild Dog: African Wild dogs live in family groups called packs. When babies are born, the whole pack helps raise the pups. When the pack goes hunting, dogs take turns staying home to guard the pups. Unlike most pack animals, these dogs share food equally with all family members.

Zebra: Zebras live in close family groups called herds. When running from danger, the herd will never leave a family member behind. If one zebra is too slow or weak, the whole family will form a circle to protect it from danger.

Penguins: There are 17 kinds of penguins. Penguins are birds but they cannot fly! Instead, they are great swimmers. With most penguins, both parents will lay on the egg to help keep it warm and then will care for the baby once it hatches.

Squirrel Monkeys: Squirrel monkeys live in Central and South America. They almost always stay in the trees. Like all monkeys, they have a tail but they can't use it to grab or hold branches. It's more to help them keep their balance while they climb. They eat fruit, nuts, seeds, insects and small birds, as well as rodents like mice and rats. They even eat bird eggs.

Catfish: Catfish live in almost all of the rivers, ponds, lakes, swamps and oceans of the world. The sharp spike on the catfish fin helps protect it from anything that tries to eat it. Catfish are also scavengers. They eat just about anything they can find. Catfish will eat other fish, dog food, bread and even chicken – the stinkier the better!

Sloth Bears: The sloth bear has very long claws. These help sloth bears dig into the dirt and tree stumps to find insects to eat. Since these bears have almost no teeth, they suck insects up through their mouth, making a slurping sound that can be heard from many miles away.

Lions: Lions are cats, big cats. They can be found in Africa and parts of Asia. They are the only cat that lives in family groups. The groups can have more than 20 members. Females do most of the hunting for the family, while male lions keep the family safe from other predators.

Y: Skills Card

Reader: _____ Room: _____

Benchmarks

Benchmarks	Date	Date
1. Read the book alone.		
2. Use the picture for clues.		
3. Pay attention to the first letter of the word.		
4. Start with the sound of the first letter.		
5. Use the picture and the first letter to figure out the word.		
6. Tell what the book was about.		
7. Break a word up into its sounds. (/b/ /a/ /t/)		
8. Read at home every night.		

I know the sound for

b	c	d
f	g	h
j	k	l
m	n	p
r	s	t
v	w	z

Can you match the pictures to the words?

snake

monkey

sheep

pig

duck

16

Gina Zorzi
Author

Trace Taylor
Photographer

Gina has always been a lover of books, but she had trouble making the transition from being read to to reading on her own. Beginning books like this one helped her learn to read. Ever since, Gina has been an avid reader. In school she would read under her desk in class, in the hallways, and even while climbing stairs. In making this book, Gina spent a lot of time carrying a very heavy tripod around several zoos and even more time waiting for Trace to take the pictures. Gina learned many amazing things about animals and now knows every comfortable spot to read at the zoo.

Some of Trace's favorite modes of transportation include her big sailboat, her cherry-red motorcycle, and her surfboards. Sadly, she no longer has any of these flashy items. Now, Trace lives in Philadelphia, where the most exciting thing she drives is a beat-up Ford. Now she gets her excitement from getting as close as she can to gross bugs and scary animals.

ARC PRESS Books

Printed with *100% New Wind Energy* and low VOC vegetable based inks

1-59301-436-8
978-1-59301-436-0

9 781593 014360